D0532314

PRAYERS
FOR THE
SEASONS
OF LIFE

PRAYERS
FOR THE
SEASONS
OF LIFE

Sue Downing
Illustrated by Ann Harsh Linebaugh

PROVIDENCE HOUSE PUBLISHERS
Franklin, Tennessee

All Bible references are from the New Revised Standard Version Bible, copyright 1989, by the Division of Christian Education of the National Council of the Churches of Christ in the United States of America.

Printed in the United States of America

01   00   99   98   5   4   3   2

Library of Congress Catalog Card Number: 97–66954

ISBN: 1–57736–041–9

"Hand in Hand" from *Alive Now!*, March/April, 1991. "Lord, We Come" from *Alive Now!*, May/June, 1996. "Here I Am, I Will Try" from *Children's Teacher*, Fall, 1996. Copyright © 1996 by Cokesbury. Used by permission. "Listen to the Children" from *Children's Leader*, Summer, 1994. Copyright © by Graded Press. Used by permission.

Painting by Ann Harsh Linebaugh; cover layout by Bozeman Design.

PROVIDENCE HOUSE PUBLISHERS
238 Seaboard Lane • Franklin, Tennessee 37067
800-321-5692

This book is dedicated with much love to my husband, Jim, and our children, Julie and Scottie.

Contents

Foreword

While serving as pastor of Brentwood United Methodist Church I asked Sue Downing to write the corporate prayers for the Sunday morning service of worship for the Advent season. I made this request because I knew that she was a prayerful person and that she had the rare ability to reduce prayers to the printed page. I also knew that she was in touch with the life and pathos of the congregation in such a way that she could help people speak with their lips what they already felt in their hearts.

Sue answered my request by writing a series of prayers for the congregation which enabled almost two thousand worshipers to pray collectively and pray with one another in a way that transcended normal experience. Again and again worshipers expressed their profound appreciation for having had the opportunity to pray through the prayers that Sue had so lovingly created for the believers of Brentwood United Methodist Church. These fixed prayers helped our people point beyond themselves to the

God who is far beyond us and yet deep within us. This was a time when our congregation needed prayers which would help us reflect upon all of life from the vantage point of the Christian faith.

Because of my relationship with Sue and my knowledge of her prayer life, I enthusiastically commend this book to the reader. Sue has captured both the meaning of prayer and also the need to pray through the various seasons and experiences of life. This book will enrich the life of reflection, meditation, and prayer for both the mature and the new Christian.

In my judgment the time has come for a book such as this. "For everything there is a season . . ." and this is *the time* for *this book* which will enable the prayer life of the church to come alive in ways that are personal, corporate, global, and universal.

After you have read this book, you will want to express a profound gratitude to Sue Downing for making this contribution to the spiritual life of the Christian church.

> Joe E. Pennel Jr., Resident Bishop
> Virginia Conference
> United Methodist Church
> February 1, 1997

Preface

This book is a gift to you, dear friends, from my heart. It is an answer to prayer and the realization of a dream I have had for a long time. Let me share with you the story of how PRAYERS FOR THE SEASONS OF LIFE came into being.

I did not set out to be an author. Although I had always enjoyed writing, this was not originally one of my personal goals. That all changed on March 5, 1979, with the birth of our son Scottie. Scottie was born with spina bifida and had this neurological disease in its severest form. Our precious infant son lived for only twenty-nine days. Without speaking a word he touched the lives of many, including my own, and eighteen years later the ripples of love still continue to flow from his brief life. The writing and publication of this book is one of them.

After Scottie's death I began to write for my own therapy. It was such a release to express my feelings. I wrote about the pain, shock, loneliness, and denial I felt. But most of all, I found myself writing about the overwhelming love Jim, Julie, and I received during this time through other people. It was a love that sustained and healed. It was God's unconditional love; a love that instilled within me the deep desire to somehow return all the love I had received. My prayer became, "Use me, Lord!"

Eventually I wrote an article, "Outpouring of Love," about our family's experience to help others going through similar crises. Out of that effort grew special writing opportunities with children's church school curricula through the United Methodist Publishing House and the publication of my first book, *Listening to Children*. Through it all, I continued to pray for God's guidance and the courage to follow God's will for my life.

About six years ago I sensed God's call to write prayers. The collection of prayers you will read in this book is my response to that call. They evolved over a lengthy period of time, under varied circumstances, and are an expression of my heart.

May God bless you and may you feel God's loving presence throughout the seasons of life.

Acknowledgments

The loving touch of many people have made PRAYERS FOR THE SEASONS OF LIFE a reality. Thank you, Ann Linebaugh, for the gift of your charming illustrations that so enhance this book. Sally Bailey, what would I have done without your adept computer skills to give form and order to my manuscript? How I appreciate all the time and effort you have devoted to this book. A big hug to the women in my Wednesday morning Bible study, who, for four years, have continued to offer me their prayers and encouragement for my writing. God bless you! Much thanks to Bishop Joe Pennel, my former pastor, for his wise guidance and the special writing opportunities he offered me at Brentwood United Methodist Church. I will be forever grateful to the staff at Providence House Publishers whose expert skills fit together "all the pieces" to create a beautiful finished product. You are a joy to work with!

PRAYERS FOR THE SEASONS OF LIFE could not have come into being without the love and support of my entire family. I lift up a very special thanks to my husband and children. Jim, thank you for standing by me, believing in me, and helping me to believe in myself. I could not ask for a better husband. Julie, thank you for being my daughter and friend. Thank you for listening. Thank you for loving. I am so proud of you. Scottie, my precious son, your life was the beginning of my writing. Through you God's love was revealed to me in a way I had never experienced it before. You live in my heart. Jim, Julie, Scottie, we are family, and I love each of you very much.

Lord, you have blessed my life abundantly.

Thanks and praise to you for the gift of my writing.

Thanks and praise to you for the gift of each person who has helped give birth to this book.

Thanks and praise to you for the gift of your love.

Amen.

PRAYERS
FOR THE
SEASONS
OF LIFE

For everything there is a season, and a time for every matter under heaven.

Ecclesiastes 3:1

A Time to
Pray

Building Bridges

Our heavenly Father, make known to us your beautiful gift of prayer.

Stifle our inner urges to place you "up there" and us "down here."

Release us from the desire to keep you at a comfortable distance.

Free us from the temptation to try and live independently from you and your will for our lives.

Protect us from the fear of drawing ever too close to you.

Take away the misconception that our thoughts, words, or actions can be hidden from your eyes.

Keep us from living a life absent of prayer.

Keep us from living a life apart from you, God.

Enlighten our hearts and minds to the real power of prayer.

Help us come to discover prayer as our personal bridge to you; a bridge that cannot be destroyed.
One whose strength grows, not weakens through use.
A bridge of communication whose foundation is built from love; a love that withstands and forever sustains.
A bridge, which through you, gives us the means to reach out to all your children.
A bridge unique to each one of us.
A bridge spanning infinity.

Lord,
Empower each of us to build our bridges.
Empower each of us to live our entire lives as prayers to you.
Amen.

A Time to
Hurt

God's People Weep

Lord, I am hurting.

I see so much suffering around me.

There is a deep yearning within me to instantly make everything all right.

Futilely, I seek the exact words or action that will immediately erase tragedy.

Frustration, helplessness, and sadness permeate my entire being.

Questions fill my mind.

Why this family? Why those people? Why my friend? Why these children? Why? Why?

Lord, I am hurting.

Help me to remember that you anguish with me and all those who suffer.

Impress on my heart that you, and you alone, are the great healer . . .

That it is only when I faithfully and willingly turn to you that I can become your instrument.

For you, Lord, have the power to put me where I need to be, give me words or keep me silent, and instill within me the desire for loving acts.

Lord, I am hurting for all the people who are hurting.
Embrace and sustain them with your love.
Bless them with renewed hope and purpose.
Show me how I can minister to their needs with the special
    gifts you have given me.

Lord, I am hurting for all the people who are hurting.
Thanks and praise be to you that no one has to bear their
    burdens alone!
Amen.

A Time to
Give

Hand in Hand

Lord, here are our hands:
Put in deep pockets to keep them safe.
Held behind our backs to keep them hidden from you.
Placed over our eyes to blind ourselves to the needs of
   others.
Buried within sand where they are immobilized and
   useless.
Patting ourselves on the back to take credit for all we are
   and do.
Grabbing for the material things of life.
Forever pushing you away.

Lord, here are your hands:
Tireless and always there for us.
Beckoning us to come closer.
Holding us secure.
Lifting us up when we are down.
Opening new doors for us.
Revealing special gifts you have given us.
Showing the way to eternal life.
Touching us with overwhelming love.
We are never the same again.

Lord, we place our hands in yours.
Take them to use as you will.
No others can touch in quite the same way as we.

Lord, hand in hand with you, we are:
Reaching out in love to others.
Inviting all to experience the abundant life.
Receiving much more than we give.
Lord, alone our hands are weak, but together, with yours,
    they are strong.
Amen.

A Time to
Follow

Follow the Star

Lord, you invite us to follow the star.
Where is it? We cannot see it.
Our vision is clouded from desiring more money and
material things, keeping track of social engagements
we have, criticizing what everyone else is doing
wrong, seeking out the influential people, looking for
means of self-gratification.
We cannot follow the star.

Lord, you invite us to follow the star.
We really do not have the time. We are very busy.
We have meetings to attend, extra hours to work, over
scheduled children to transport, clubs to join, dead-
lines to meet, and countless other commitments.
We cannot follow the star.

Lord, you invite us to follow the star.
We are afraid.
What will happen to us along the way? How much risk is
involved? What is in it for us? How long do we
follow? What is at the end of our journey?
We do not like the unknown. We want everything in black
and white.
We cannot follow the star.

Lord, you invite us to follow the star.

We are really not qualified.

Why not leave us alone and ask others? I am sure they could do far better than any of us, and following the star is really not "our thing."

We cannot follow the star.

Lord, you invite us to follow the star.

What is this? You still want us after all our excuses? You love us and promise to be with us now and forever? You will never give up on us? You are waiting patiently for us?

We will try to follow the star.

Lord, you invite us to follow the star.

With your loving guidance we cautiously take the first steps. We begin to reach out in love to others. We give of ourselves. Each expression of love makes the star shine brighter and draws us closer to you.

Look, we can see the star!

Lord, you invite us to follow the star.

It leads us to a manger in Bethlehem, where love was born. Help us to know that the star is in us and shines within our hearts. Help us to live our lives in such a way that others can see your love shining radiantly through us.

Thank you for the gift of love and the awesome privilege and responsibility it brings.

Lord, you invite us to follow the star.
Joy to the world!
Amen.

A Time to
Gather

Lord, We Come

Lord, we come.
We eagerly anticipate growing together in our faith through
your Word.
We search for answers. What is your will for my life?
What are my gifts? What meaning does the Bible have for
me?

Lord, we come.
But we hesitate. We are not quite sure what to expect.
Questions haunt our minds. What will be asked of me?
Who is this person at my side? Do I really want to be
here?
What if? What if? What if?

Lord, we come.
Deep within us is the real need and desire to be here.
We cannot ignore your call to be faithful. We say *yes* in
obedient response to your invitation. We submit to
your patient prodding.
We know the choice is ours.

Lord we come.
We bring with us our hopes, fears, doubts, beliefs, questions,
needs, gifts, differences, experiences.
We bring our uniqueness, our specialness. We bring ourselves, and the knowledge that each of our lives is a
gift from you.

Lord, we come.

We claim your promise that "where two or three are gathered in my name, I am there among them."

We rest in the assurance that we are not alone.

We know you brought us together for a purpose, and we are thankful.

We affirm your loving presence with us.

Lord, we come.

We come, so that we can go "into the world and make disciples of all nations,

Baptizing them in the name of the Father, Son, and Holy Spirit."

Amen.

A Time to
Witness

The Church Doors Open,

Lord,
The church doors open.

We enter . . . dressed in our finest, smiles on our faces, words of kindness on our lips, and Bibles in our hands.

We sit piously in our pews, listening to your Word, singing your praises, praying reverently to you, and offering our gifts, all at the proper time.

We recite the Lord's Prayer, profess what we believe, kneel at your altar, eat bread and drink wine at your table, baptize our children, and receive the blessing of the benediction.

We go from our pews, greeting those around us, welcoming new members, shaking the minister's hand, and saying to ourselves, "What a good person I am!"

Lord,
The church doors close.

We leave to go to our homes, schools, neighborhoods, businesses, communities.

We say one thing and practice another.

We place ourselves in the center.

We count our worth by material things.

We seek friendships for our own gain.

The Church Doors Close

We go along with the crowd.
We seek recognition for our good works.
We remain blind to those hurting around us.
Sunday after Sunday, the church doors open.
Week after week, the church doors close.

Lord,
Your arms are patiently there for us.
You embrace us with your love.
Not when it is convenient, to impress, or prove a point.
Not only on Sundays, but each moment of every day.
Not because we deserve it, but because you love us far
    more than we can ever know.
Impress your love on our hearts.
Instill in us the desire to be instruments of this love
    wherever we are and to glorify your name in all we do.
Let each one of us remember that we are your children
    and your arms in the world.

Lord,
The church doors open. The church doors close.
Help us to be true Christians.
Help us to keep the doors open wide, that your love might
    flow from within to without, without to within.
Amen.

A Time to
Grow

The Circle

One by one, week after week, we come.
Individuals who are drawn together for a single
purpose—to grow in our faith.
Each person brings a uniqueness.
Each person offers special gifts.
One by one, week after week, we go.

One by one, week after week, we come.
The *I's* become *We*.
We study, question, share, and pray.
We bear each others' burdens.
We celebrate each others' joys.
We dream each others' dreams.
One by one, week after week, we go.

One by one, week after week, we come.
Hands reach out to touch
Hands reach out to welcome.
Hands reach out for Christ.
One by one, week after week, we go.

One by one, week after week, we come.
We are a circle.
A circle whose strength depends on each person.
A circle willing to move, bend, and grow!
A circle with God at the center.
A circle bound together by love.
One by one, week after week, we go.

One by one, week after week, we come.
And whether we come or whether we go,
Our circle of love remains unbroken.
God's Holy Spirit unites our hearts as one!
Praise and thanks be to God!

A Time to
Begin Anew

Endings and Beginnings

Dear God,

We come before you with joy and thanksgiving for the dawning of a new year.

As we look towards the future and the limitless possibilities that are before us, we ask for your loving guidance in whatever lies ahead.

Help us to clearly envision what your will is for each one of your children, and give us the courage to strive towards the dreams you set before us.

Make us keenly aware that whatever challenges, whatever trials we have to face, you are there beside us.

Lead us to the realization that life is a precious gift not to be taken lightly or thoughtlessly abused.

Forgive us for those all too familiar sins and those sins we choose to ignore, that we commit over and over again.

Impress on us the understanding that you are not a God of force, but a God who patiently directs us and allows us to make our own choices.

Grant us the knowledge that each moment of every day is a new beginning, and because of you and the gift of your Son, Jesus Christ, we can face all our tomorrows with the promise of renewed hope and carry the light of that hope into all the world.

Amen.

A Time to
Give Thanks

A Thankful Heart

Lord,

My heart overflows with thanksgiving as I experience times of joy.

I readily offer thanks to you for . . .

There is no cancer.
Yes, the job is yours.
You have a healthy baby boy.
The verdict is not guilty.
Your loved one survived the accident.
The award belongs to you.
Those spontaneous moments of family closeness.
The precious gift of a lasting friendship.
A star-filled sky.
The beauty of the changing seasons.
A misunderstanding resolved.
A prayer answered "my way."
Supportive words directed towards me.
An addictive habit overcome.

The time for a thankful heart is now.
I can see the blessings.
I can feel the blessings.

Lord,

My heart is empty of thanksgiving as times of deep hurt and sadness engulf me.

I cannot conceive of giving thanks for these crises and setbacks in my life.

The possibility barely enters my mind.

Negative feelings dominate my thoughts and actions.

The question "Why me Lord?" becomes my daily prayer.

I feel isolated and alone.

These are times for no thankful heart.

I cannot see the blessings.

A barrier of my own design blocks the blessings.

Lord,

Fill my heart with thanksgiving in every circumstance of life as only you can do.

Look beyond my humanness.

Touch me with your love which encompasses and transcends all things.

Instill within me the desire to give thanks in times of sadness as well as times of joy.

Affirm your presence with me.

Lead me to the belief that the time for a thankful heart is always.

Give me the faith to know that through you my eyes will open to see and my heart will open to receive the countless blessings you want to bestow on me in all things.

Lord,

Thanks and praise to you for my life and whatever it holds for me.

Amen.

A Time to
Receive

The Gift

God, you offer each of us a gift.
We are chosen to receive this gift.
It is freely given to us.
The gift is wrapped in hope and tied securely with love.

God, you offer each of us a gift.
It is ours and ours alone to receive.
Each gift is unique and special.
With it comes the awesome privilege and responsibility of
    choosing what we do with our gift.

God, you offer each of us a gift.
Many do not recognize it as one.
We do not even acknowledge there is a giver.
"I am who I am, because of me!" we emphatically state.
"I deserve everything I have got!"

God, you offer each of us a gift.
There are those who say, "I do not like my gift. I want
    another one. Mine is too big, little, plain, fancy, inex-
    pensive, the wrong color, or too difficult to use.
Let me have one of those gifts over there. They look much
    better."

God, you offer each of us a gift.

Some of us hoard our gift. We hide it in a deep, dark corner where no one else can find it and no light can shine upon it.

We fear our gift will be discovered. We selfishly guard from having to share it with anyone.

God, you offer each of us a gift.

Many receivers abuse their gift. "It is mine forever. I can treat it any way I want!"

Slowly, these gifts deteriorate until they become useless.

God, you offer me a gift.

Help me to look within my gift to see Jesus.

Help me to see an empty tomb and believe.

Help me to look at the cross, touch Jesus' nail-pierced hands, and know that my sins are forgiven.

God, you offer me a gift.

Help me to know my gift was bought with the price of your Son, Jesus Christ.

Instill in me the desire and courage to use my gift to "go make disciples."

God, you offer me a gift.

It is the gift of my life.

It is the gift of abundant, everlasting life.

Alleluia! Alleluia!

Amen.

A Time to
Hope

Good Friday in My Heart

Lord, it is Good Friday in my heart.

Darkness permeates everything around me and seeps into my very being.

I am engulfed in disbelief and pain.

I cry out in my frustration and anger, "Why me, Lord? What have I done to deserve this?"

The burden is far too heavy.

The loneliness I feel is much more than I can bear.

My life is reduced to "going through the motions."

Surely I will "awake" to discover this is all a bad dream.

Lord, it is Good Friday in my heart.

But yesterday a friend listened with care, and a stranger took time to comfort me.

Today my neighbor reached out with a healing touch, and someone offered a prayer in my name.

Acts of lovingkindness somehow ease the emptiness.

The deep sense of hurt remains, but love has slowly found its place too.

There is a glimpse of a rainbow in the distance!

Lord, the dawning of renewed hope is in my heart.

I am increasingly aware of the gift of your presence.

My faith in you gradually moves me from darkness towards the light, from utter despair towards wholeness.

Day by day, step by step, I begin to claim your promise of abundant life.

Lord, the dawning of renewed hope is in my heart.
I can face the cross and know that your love transcends all
things.
I can face the cross and rest in the assurance that I am
never alone.
I can face the cross and believe that all things work
together for good when we place our trust in you.

Lord, it is Easter morning in my heart.
The stone is rolled away, and the tomb is empty.
Christ is risen!
Love has triumphed over evil!

Lord, it is Easter morning in my heart.
Alleluia! Alleluia!
Amen.

A Time to
Listen

Listen to the Children

Listen to the children.
They are the future of the church but also very much the
now of the church.
Listen to the children.
They are loving, trusting, growing, and becoming.
Listen to the children.
They seek guidance and learn by example.
Their hands reach out to grasp and to give.
Listen to the children.
Each child is a special gift from God. How they need our
love!
Listen to the children.
In so doing, we will discover how very much we need
them.

A Time to
Prepare

Journey through Advent
Look Beyond

Dear God,

As we begin our journey through this Advent season,

Open our eyes that we might look beyond the glitz and commercialism of the world and see hope.

Open our ears that we might listen and hear your words of promise in a world of pain and suffering.

Open our mouths that we might proclaim your message of joy to a world divided and in need.

Open our arms that we might reach out to embrace the lonely and outcasts of this world.

Open our hearts that we might be so filled with your Spirit that it overflows into every corner of our world.

Sensitize our whole being that we might be fully prepared to receive your great gift of love to the world.

Take our hands and lead us step by step to a manger in Bethlehem.

For we know Christ is coming. Christ is coming indeed!

Amen.

Journey through Advent
Take Time

Dear God,

In the midst of his holy Advent season, we pray that you might guide us to take time in our waiting.

Help us to focus our thoughts on you and your will for our lives.

Let us be aware of your loving presence and how you forever dwell within us.

Impress on our hearts the responsibility and privilege we have of sharing our faith so others may come to believe and find inner peace.

Make us still during the hurriedness of these days so we can listen to the needs of others and respond to them in love.

Awaken in us the joy of spending special moments with family, friends, and you, Lord.

Take our hands and lead us step by step to a manger in Bethlehem.

For we know Christ is coming. Christ is coming indeed!
Amen.

Journey through Advent
Travel Light

Dear God,

As we experience Advent, a sacred time of preparation,
help us to travel light along the way.

Instill in us the desire to shed the bonds of materialism,
self-gratification, and prejudice from our lives.

Subdue our anger, resentment, impatience, and apathy.

Eliminate all the unnecessary busyness of each day.

Cleanse us of our sins, and give each of us the courage and
strength to rid ourselves of those things which are
unacceptable to you.

Make us aware that there is no room for anything or
anyone but you, God, at the center of our lives.

Take our hands and lead us step by step to a manger in
Bethlehem.

For we know Christ is coming. Christ is coming indeed!

Amen.

Journey through Advent
Remember

Dear God,

In the remaining days of our Advent journey, a special time of great expectancy, help us to remember.

Direct our thoughts towards the countless blessings you have bestowed on each one of us.

Forever remind us that we belong to you, and the love you have for your children remains constant and unconditional.

Let us never forget that the essence of all we are and ever hope to be we owe to you.

Give us thankful hearts for the precious gift of life to be cherished always.

Hold deep within each of us the memories of those faithful who have gone before us to illuminate and show us the way.

Help us to remember that without our faith in you, our lives become immobile and useless.

Take our hands and lead us step by step to the manger in Bethlehem.

For we know Christ is coming. Christ is coming indeed!

Amen.

A Time to
Be Joyful

Kneeling at the Manger

Dear God,

On this Christmas Day we gather together around a lowly manger in Bethlehem to celebrate with joy and thanksgiving the birth of your Son, Jesus Christ.

We rejoice with one another that the culmination of our Advent journey marks not an ending, but the promise of a new beginning for all of mankind.

We gaze into the face of a tiny baby and see the Savior for a troubled world.

We fall on our knees in praise and adoration that you would send your Son to live and walk among us.

We humbly offer to you the gift of ourselves in grateful response for the love that was born today.

Take our hands and lead us step by step from a manger in Bethlehem,

To proclaim with the angels over all the earth, "Joy to the world!"

Christ has come. Christ has come indeed!

Amen.

A Time to
Risk

Leaving the Familiar

Lord,
I cling tightly to the familiar.
There is comfort in the expected;
Security in the known.
I resist treading on uncharted ground.
I stand firmly on my spot in life.

Why risk change?
You challenge me to let go of the familiar;
To shed my feelings of fear and inadequacy.
Gently and persistently your Spirit prods me to move on.
I search for guarantees. I want proof for success.

Why risk change?
Help me to release my grip on the familiar.
Grant me the trust to move forward with confidence on
    the path you have set for me.
Implant in my heart the knowledge that your loving
    presence upholds me in all circumstances of life.
I feel your touch. I need only to reach out to you. The
    decision is mine.

Why risk change?

Because to remain forever in the familiar leads to stagnation and death,

But to depart from the familiar with God's guidance results in growth and life.

How can I not risk change?

Amen.

A Time to
Be Still

Slow Me Down, Lord

Slow me down, Lord.
I have placed myself on "fast forward"
    and completely lost control.
My life is a myriad of scheduled activities,
    commitments, and mounting responsibilities, that
    have lost all significance for me.

Slow me down, Lord.
Day after day I find myself going through the motions
    of someone I think I need to be.
Yet this person I have become is out of order and
    does not function anymore.

Slow me down, Lord.
I have propelled myself into a dark hole and cannot
    find the way out.
It is a cold, lonely place, and I am desperately searching
    for direction and meaning out of this chaos.

Slow me down, Lord.
Deep within my being I sense a longing to discover and
    release the real me.
I try to imagine what special gifts I possess which lie
    dormant, waiting to emerge.

Slow me down, Lord.
I am so impatient and speed oriented.
I live moment upon moment, day after day looking
for shortcuts and the easier path to anywhere and
everywhere.

Slow me down, Lord.
Wrap your loving arms around me so that I can feel the
warmth of your touch within my heart.
Instill in me the desire to respond to your call.

Slow me down, Lord.
Enable me to be still and know that you are God.
Give me the courage and strength to wait and turn the
control of my life over to you.

Slow me down, Lord.
So that together we can "give birth" to the beautiful
creature you would have me become!

Slow me down, Lord.
Give me time to grow!
Amen.

A Time to
Become as Children

Awaken the Child within Me

Lord,

Awaken the child within me.

Let me look upon your world with a renewed sense of awe and wonder.

Give me the eyes of a child so that I can experience the miracles of creation as if for the first time.

Awaken the child within me.

Let me step out into your world and live my life with a quiet trust in things unseen.

Grant me the feet of a child so that I can walk in faith with the constant assurance that you are guiding me.

Awaken the child within me.

Let me reach out into your world and minister to each of your children freely and unconditionally.

Bestow on me the arms of a child so that I can wrap them around a troubled world and be a witness of your everlasting love for us.

Awaken the child within me.

Let me gaze upon the face of baby Jesus, your Light to the world.

Give me the heart of a child so that the promise of hope is rekindled anew.

Awaken the child within me.

Let me recapture the true essence of wonder, faith, love, and hope!

Let me discover and enter the kingdom of God.

Amen.

A Time to
Decide

The Choice

Dear Lord,
We are people.
We are children, parents, relatives, singles, spouses, neighbors, friends, coworkers, leaders, followers, club joiners, church members, students, volunteers.
And the list goes on.
We are who we are.
And each new day, who we are for that moment, that day, determines the decisions we must make.

We are challenged:
> To give or take.
>> To go or stay.
> To forgive or seek revenge.
>> To accept or deny.
> To touch or withdraw.
>> To take the time or be too busy.
> To share or withhold.
>> To listen or talk.
> To encourage or criticize.
>> To appreciate or take for granted.
> To hope or despair.
>> To love or hate.

And the list goes on.

Dear Lord,
We are people.
 We are your children.
  We are special and unique.
  We are, because of you.
And each new day, who we are for that moment, that day,
 is determined by one decision, which is ours alone to
 make.

We are given the choice:
To follow you and search out your will for our lives or to
 follow ourselves and rely on our own resources.
And the list stops here.
For to choose one is to choose abundant life. To choose
 the other is to choose death.
Amen.

A Time to
Dream

Dreams

Lord, we pray.

We share our dreams with you.

These dreams are as varied and unique as the number of people here.

But they are unified through one purpose.

That purpose is to lovingly minister to the needs of this world for your glory.

Lord, we listen.

Help us to know in our hearts if our dreams are truly your dreams for us too.

Guide us in the understanding that with your loving guidance and our willingness to serve, we have the power to accomplish anything.

Instill in us the courage to pursue our dreams with a confident and perserverant spirit.

Lord, we act.

We affirm your presence in our lives.

We claim your promise that, "He who believes in me will also do the works that I do; and greater works than these will he do, because I go to the Father."

We strive to make our dreams a reality.

Step by step we become aware that you have far greater plans and blessings for us than we can begin to imagine.

Lord, we give thanks.

For with you anything is possible,

But without you we are nothing!

Amen.

A *Time to*
Teach

Be with Me

Lord,

Be with me as I teach.

Let your abiding presence permeate all the things that I do.

I pray for guidance in my words as well as my silence.

Give me direction in every move that I make, every action that I take.

Create within me a caring heart and the deep desire to share the best of myself with others.

May I come to the belief that every day overflows with opportunities for teaching.

Keep in my memory the vision of your Son, Jesus, the master teacher, and the everlasting lessons he continues to teach.

Impart to me the real need to be a living example of Christ's love to your children.

Be with those whom I teach.

Thank you for bringing them into my life.

Praise to you for the many blessings that are mine because of their touch.

Help me to be forever aware that through teaching I become the learner;

Through giving, I become the receiver.

Lord,
Be with me as I teach.
Be with me as I learn.
Be with me as I strive to draw ever nearer to you and the
realization of your will for my life.
Amen.

A Time to
Live

Live Life

Lord, you give us life.

Help each of us to cherish this precious gift of love and
realize what a priceless treasure we have.

Guide us in the understanding that our existence is not
measured by the number of hours, days, or years
spent on this earth.

Release us from the belief that our true value is determined
by the amount of our material possessions.

Free us from the illusion that each award, word of praise,
or accolade that we receive increases our worth.

Erase from our minds the feeling that outward
appearances impress more than what is visible within.

Lord, you give us life.

Show us how to fully embrace it.

Open our hearts to the endless blessings life can hold.

Give us the knowledge that lives are shaped moment by
moment and how we choose to spend those moments
we have.

Keep our eyes focused on your Son Jesus who . . .

> Was born in a stable
> Healed the sick
> Ate with tax collectors
> Reached out to the poor
> Welcomed the children
> Forgave his accusers
> Followed God's will
> Prayed to his heavenly Father
> Died so that we might have eternal life.

Lord, you give us life.
May we always remember the source of our gift and live
our lives as gifts of thankful response to you.
Amen.

A Time to
Love

I Am Called

Lord, you have called me to minister to others.
To reach out in love and support to your children,
To listen with a caring heart and be a friend to those in
    need,
To give the gift of my time.
Lord, you have called me to minister to others.
Instill within my heart the knowledge that whatever I have
    to offer, you can multiply and make wonderful.
Erase my fears of inadequacy and help me focus on the
    importance of doing your work in a hurting world.
Lord, you have called me to minister to others.
I say *yes* in thankful response for all the love I have
    received.
I say *yes* with the blessed assurance that you will be with
    me every step of the way.
Lord, you have called me to minister to others.
What a blessing and privilege it is!
Amen.

A Time to
Forgive

A Heavy Heart

Lord, my heart is heavy.

Feelings of bitterness, resentment, anger, and fear weigh me down.

The burden is more than I can bear;

The hurt overwhelming.

I cling tightly to the belief that I am the one betrayed.

I am the victim.

There is no room for forgiveness; no place for love.

Peace eludes me.

Why should I reach out?

Why is it my responsibility to move towards reconciliation?

The blame is not mine; it belongs to another.

Lord, cleanse my heart.

Replace the negative feelings with compassion.

Fill me with the realization that we are all your children.

Give me the desire and humility to forgive.

Impart to me the faith to know you walk with me in all circumstances.

Lord, illuminate my heart.

Kneel with me at your communion table as I partake of the bread and wine, your body broken for me, your blood poured out for me.

Awaken in me again the truth that you gave your Son, Jesus, for my sins.

Impress on my heart that we forgive, because you first forgave us.

Lord, I go now to forgive.

The burden is lifted; my heart is light.

Amen.

A Time to
Serve

Here I Am—I Will Try

Lord, you have called me to minister in a way I never have
before.
I feel so inadequate for this task.
My qualifications are few, and my reasons to say *no* are
many.
Are you sure you have connected with the right person?
Maybe you need to talk with a more likely candidate. .

Lord, you have called me to minister in a way I never have
before.
I feel afraid and unsure of what to expect or what I am to
do.
What if I do not like the job I am involved with? What if
I am a failure?
What if? What if?
Lord, it is not too late to say *no,* is it?

Lord, you have called me to minister in a way I never have
before.
I am overwhelmed by the mere thought of what you have
asked me to do.
It requires considerable time and effort to walk on
unfamiliar ground.
How about letting me choose something else I can do to
help you that feels more comfortable?

Lord, you have called me to minister in a way I never have before.

You say you will be with me each step of the way.

You ask me to remember Moses and countless others who thought they were the wrong persons to serve.

You remind me that I am the one you want in spite of all my excuses.

Lord, you have called me to minister in a way I never have before.

Hesitantly, I take that first step of faith.

Here I am Lord. I will try!

Amen.

A Time to
Remember

Scottie

It is Christmas time, the season of love and joy.
I think of our precious little boy.
He was sent to us from the heavens above,
A gift of the Father, carrying a message of love.
His stay was brief. He had no words to say,
But his life continues to "touch" us each and every day.
"How is this possible?" one might ask,
For someone so small to perform such a task.
The answer comes from God's love and God's grace;
It radiated like starlight from Scottie's face.
When our baby went to heaven, I knew in my heart,
That through his message of love we would never be apart.
And in remembering our Scottie, I fall on my knees,
Thanking God for an angel; what a blessing to receive!